Skyline 2

Workbook

Barbara Garside

MACMILLAN

Contents

Unit 1 Activate your English

1 At an international convention

1 Pronunciation work

a Put the letters in the correct column depending on their sound.

a b c d e f g h i j k l m n o p q r s t u v w x y z

day	be		get	my	go	you	are
a	b						

b Now say the rhyming letters to yourself.

c Spell out these words aloud to yourself.

> airplane   English   Jamaica   Italian   convention   registration
> international   welcome   payment   cocktail

Language summary: saying what you do

Use:	Form:		
To be + *a* / *an* + job.	I	'm	a student.
(*a* before a consonant and *an* before a vowel)	You	're	an electrician.
I'm a doctor.	He	's	a driver.
He's an engineer.	She	's	an accountant.

2 Language work

a Write sentences about these people.

> **Language note**
>
> To say where you work, use *at* or *in* (usually *in* when you are talking generally and *at* when you give more information or the name).
>
> *I work **in** a school / factory / hospital.*
>
> but *I work **at** a New York State hospital. I work **at** IBM.*

REGISTRATION FORM

Name: Rosario Lopez

Country of origin: Guatemala

Occupation:
Compter software designer

Place of work: Microsoft

REGISTRATION FORM

Name: Steve Hardy

Country of origin: Australia

Occupation:
Journalist

Place of work: REUTERS

REGISTRATION FORM

Name: Franz Schwimmer

Country of origin: Germany

Occupation:
Engineer

Place of work: T & T

REGISTRATION FORM

Name: Rossana Toriano

Country of origin: Italy

Occupation:
Doctor

Place of work: Milan Children's Hospital

1 Rosario's from Guatemala. She's a computer software designer. She works at Microsoft.

2 ....

3 ....

4 ....

b Put the conversation in the correct order.

I'm an English teacher.	....	I'm from Trinidad.	....
Where do you work?	....	I work at Port-of-Spain University.	....
What do you do?	....	Where are you from?	...1...

2 In a foreign city

Language summary: where you live / work / are from			
Use:		**Form:**	

Use:
- Use the present simple tense to talk about where you live / work / are from. *I live in Santiago.*
- Don't forget to add *-s* for he and she. *He **works** at the construction company.*
- Use *don't* and *doesn't* for negative sentences. *They **don't come** from Washington.* *She **doesn't work** in a clinic.*

Form:

I / You / We / They	live	in New York.
He / She	lives	
I / You / We / They	don't	live in San Francisco.
He / She	doesn't	

1 Language work

Correct the mistakes in these sentences.

He walk to school. <u>He walks to school.</u>

1 She work in an auto plant. ....

2 He don't live in London. ....

3 I from Hong Kong. ....

4 They doesn't live in Seattle. ....

5 He no work in a technical college. ....

2 Skills work: writing

Think about someone you know and write a short paragraph like this.

<u>Her name's Susi. She's my cousin. She doesn't live here. She lives in Bangkok and she works in a</u> ....
<u>translation agency.</u> ....

....

....

3 Skills work: reading

a Read about Sydney and write down two facts you have learned about the city.

<u>Sydney is famous for its wonderful food.</u>

1 ....

....

....

2 ....

....

....

SYDNEY

One of the best known and most beautiful cities in Australia is Sydney. Many people think of it as the capital though the capital is in fact Canberra. Sydney is on the southeast coast of Australia, in New South Wales. It is famous for its Opera House, its wonderful food and its spectacular beaches. Sydney is a very cosmopolitan city with inhabitants from all over the world, including Vietnamese, Turkish, Greek and many other nationalities. The main languages, apart from English, are Italian, Greek and Aboriginal languages.

In the year 2000, the Olympic Games were held in Sydney and many people thought they were the best Games ever.

b Write complete sentences in answer to the questions.

Where is Sydney?

It's on the southeast coast of Australia. / It's in New South Wales.

1 What is it famous for?

2 What different nationalities live there?

3 What languages do they speak?

4 What do people do on weekends?

5 What happened in 2000 in Sydney?

c Correct the mistakes.

Sydney is in Queensland.

It isn't in Queensland. / It's in New South Wales.

1 Sydney is the capital of Australia.

2 Sydney is famous for its museums and mountains.

3 Only Australians live in Sydney.

4 Apart from English, people speak mainly French and Russian.

4 Word work: nationalities and languages

Complete the table. Use a dictionary or encyclopedia to help you and don't forget to use capital letters.

Country	Nationality	Languages
U.S.A.	American	English, Spanish
Brazil		
Holland		
Canada		
Argentina		
New Zealand		
Panama		

3 Getting to know you

Language summary: asking and answering general questions about people				
Use:	**Form:**			
• Use the simple present to ask and answer about	Where do	you / they	live?	
people: what they like / dislike, where they live / work,	I / They	live	in Sydney.	
things they do often.	What	does	he / she	do?
• Don't forget to use *do* or *does* in the question and in	He / She	teaches	in a college.	
the short answer.	Do	you / they	speak French?	
Do** you like New York? Yes, **I do.** / No, **I don't.	Does	he / she		
Does** she play tennis? Yes, she **does.** / No, she **doesn't.	Yes	I / they	do.	
	No		don't.	
	Yes	he / she	does.	
	No		doesn't.	

1 Language work

a Write answers to these questions.

Do all Australians speak English?
  Yes, they do. / No, they don't.
....

1 Is San Francisco in Washington State?
....

2 Do you speak Spanish?
....

3 Are you English?
....

4 Does your best friend live in your hometown?
....

5 Does your sister go to college?
....

b Write questions for these answers.

Yes, she does. She plays every day.
  Does she play basketball?
....

1 I speak five languages.
....

2 No, he doesn't. He hates it.
....

3 Yes, he does, but it isn't his hometown.
....

4 No, they don't. They work in a hospital.
....

5 No, I don't. I study at school.
....

c Correct the mistakes in this text.

FOSVEN
THE HOUSE MAGAZINE

The Leading Company in Chile!

WELCOME TO SANTI

Santi Gutierrez are from Chile but he live in Caracas. He marketing manager at Fosven, Caracas. He's work in the plant just outside Caracas. He like his job but he finds it quite stressful. He go running every morning and on weekends he like to swim and to play with his children. He say this help with the stress!

d Now answer these questions about Santi Gutierrez. Use short answers where possible.

Is Santi from Venezuela? *Yes, he is.* ....

1 Does he work in an office? ....

2 Does he like his job? ....

3 What does he do every morning? ....

4 What does he do on weekends? ....

5 Why does he do that? ....

2 Skills work: writing

a Write about someone you know.
Write a paragraph similar to the one about Santi, but without the mistakes!

....
....
....
....

b Now write a similar paragraph about yourself.

....
....
....
....

Unit 2 Your environment

1 A nice place to work

1 Pronunciation work

Mark the stress on these words and phrases by underlining them.

| <u>te</u>lephone   filing cabinet   scanner   work station   fax machine |

Do you notice anything about the compounds (two words together)?

2 Skills work: writing

a   Read again the text in your Student's Book about telecommuting.
Write some of the advantages and disadvantages of telecommuting in two lists like this:

Advantages	Disadvantages
flexible working hours	no contact with colleagues

b   Now use your notes to write a paragraph about the advantages and disadvantages of telecommuting.
You could start like this:

One advantage of telecommuting is that you have flexible working hours but it can be lonely because you
have little direct contact with your colleagues.

Language summary: talking about things in progress now			
Use:		**Form:**	
Use *to be* + *-ing* if what you are talking about is happening now.		I'm (I am) leaving	the office now.
		He's (He is) taking	a shower right now.
He's walking down the street toward me.			
I'm talking to my mother on the phone.			

3 Language work

a Think of someone you know whose day is different from yours and write sentences like this:

When I am getting up, she is starting work.

1 ....

2 ....

3 ....

4 ....

b Write sentences about these people.

1 He's playing basketball.

2 ....

3 ....

4 ....

5 ....

6 ....

11

Unit 2 Lesson 2

2 A nice place to live

Language summary: talking about quantities and numbers

Use:

• You can use *a lot of* in all types of sentence:
*There is **a lot of** traffic. There aren't **a lot of** stores.*
• You can use *much* with singular uncountable nouns and *many* with plural nouns in negative sentences and questions:
*There **isn't much** noise. **Are there many** restaurants?*

Form:

There	is	a lot of	noise.
	are		cars.
There	isn't	a lot of	pollution.
		much	
There	aren't	a lot of	restaurants.
		many	

• Don't forget it isn't correct to use *too much / too many* except when you think it is a bad thing or about something you are criticizing: *I really hate it here. There's **too much** noise.*
*She isn't happy in her job. There are **too many** things to do.*

1 Skills work: reading

a Read this article about Istanbul and fill in the blanks with *much*, *many* or *a lot of*.

TURKEY

Istanbul, in Turkey, is a great place to visit. There are a ....lot of........ stores, bars and restaurants. There are also (1) .... markets, mosques and other beautiful places to visit. One problem, though, is that there is (2) .... noise and (3) .... traffic. This means that there is also (4) .... pollution and sometimes it can get really bad, especially in the winter. Another problem is that there isn't (5) .... public transportation and there aren't always (6) .... taxis, but two great ways of getting around are on one of the many ferries which go back and forth across the Bosphorus or by Dolmus (which means "stuffed"), a kind of minibus in which they pack in as (7) .... people as they possibly can!

b Correct the mistakes in this text.

London is famous for its much historic buildings and museums. It really has much interesting architecture. There are also too many pubs, restaurants and clubs but the pubs close at 11 p.m. so there aren't much places to go after that. The climate is quite mixed and there is many rain but luckily there are too much things to do even when the weather is bad.

2 Skills work: writing

a Take a good look at the room you are in at the moment and write a paragraph about it, using *much*, *many* and *lots of / a lot of*.

June 15th, 4p.m.

Dear Rosa/Roberto,
I'm sitting in my room now. ....
....
....
....
....
....
....

3 Language work

a Rearrange these words and phrases to make questions.

the Windy City / nickname / New York's / is / ?
Is New York City's nickname the Windy City?
....

1 going out / on Saturday night / are you / with some friends / ?
....

2 a lot of / city / traffic / there / in your / is / ?
....

3 many / near your / house / restaurants / are there / ?
....

4 in your town / much / there / is / crime / ?
....

5 class / of the course / is your / going to have / a party at the end / ?
....

b Now answer the questions for yourself.

Is New York City's nickname the Windy City? No it isn't. It's the Big Apple.

3 A big move

Language summary: describing places
Use:
• When you are describing a place don't forget to put the adjective before the noun. adjective + noun *a busy town a big city*	• If you want to intensify or modify the adjective you can use *very* or *fairly*. *very / fairly* + adjective + noun *a **fairly** quiet town a **very** large city*

1 Word work: opposites

a Write the opposites of these words (they may not be exact opposites and sometimes there is more than one possibility).

small   ......*large*......   **3** industrial   ....

1 quiet   ....   **4** commercial   ....

2 ugly   ....   **5** slow   ....

b In these sentences write the words in the correct order.

He has hair long. ...*He has long hair.*...

1 I live in a quiet fairly town. ....

2 The area residential is big fairly. ....

3 She likes cities very big. ....

4 We have neighbors nice very and they have a yard pretty.

....

5 It is an job interesting and relaxing. ....

2 Language work

a Correct the mistakes.

This is she's book.   *her* book ....

1 He's name is Antonio.   ....

2 She aunt's name is Marta.   ....

3 I really like theirs new house.   ....

4 This is my sister. Your name is Juana.   ....

5 Are they yours teachers?   ....

> **Language note**
> Possessive adjectives describe who owns a thing, or who has a relationship to a person.
> *This is **my** sister.*
> *This is **their** car.*

b Fill in the blanks in this text using possessive adjectives.

This is a picture of ....*our*..... new house. We like it a lot
because we have (1) .... own yard and the children
have (2) .... own rooms. Susana put all (3)
.... toys in (4) .... new bedroom and Miguel
put (5) .... posters all over the walls.
We like (6) .... new neighbors and they invited us to
(7) .... house for dinner last night.
(8) .... yard is really pretty and I am hoping that
soon (9) .... yard will be as pretty as theirs.

3 Word work: where you live or work

> work station   good equipment   space   furniture   contact with people   residential
> air conditioning   agricultural   comfortable   flexible hours   quiet   take a shower
> nice neighbors   fax machine   industrial   commute   check your e-mail   filing cabinet

a Put the words / phrases in the correct column.

Where you work	Where you live	Where you work *or* live
work station	residential	furniture

b Now choose five of the words / phrases which you think are useful for you to remember and write a definition or sentence to illustrate their meaning.

.....One problem with working from home is you don't have much direct contact with people.................

1 ....

2 ....

3 ....

4 ....

5 ....

Unit 3 People in your life

1 Family matters

1 Word work: family relatives

a Look at this family tree and read the text about it.

William Boulton married Charlotte Norbury in 1945 and they had three children, two sons, Charlie and Peter, and a daughter, Caroline. In 1976, when she was 20, Caroline met Ben at college and they got married a year later. They now have two daughters, Susan and Maria. Peter married his best friend's sister, Georgie, and they have a son, Jack. Peter's brother, Charlie, never married but he is a wonderful uncle to his nephew and nieces. Susan and Maria often stay with their Uncle Peter and their Aunt Georgie and they get along very well with Jack, their only cousin. They also love visiting their grandparents, especially because they always get lots of presents.

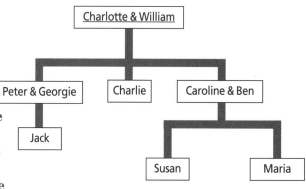

b Underline all the words for family members in the text and notice where they are on the family tree. One example has been done for you.

c Read this text and complete the family tree to illustrate it.

Elena Lopez and Jorge Fernandez got married in 1957 and had two daughters, Carmen and Teresa, and a son, also named Jorge like his father. Teresa met Roque when she went to work in Colombia for a short time and they were married two years later. They have a son, Carlos, and a baby daughter, Elenita. Jorge is married to Alicia and they have two sons, Pedro and Esteban. Alicia is expecting another baby soon and Pedro and Esteban are hoping for a sister. Carmen is not married but she loves being an aunt to her nephews, Carlos, Pedro and Esteban and her little niece, Elenita.

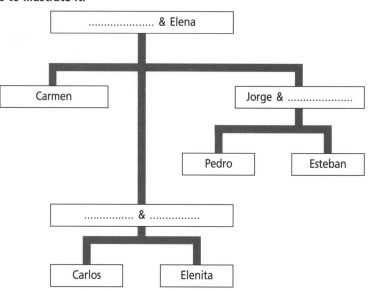

2 **Skills work:** writing 1

Now draw on a sheet of paper your own family tree. Start with your grandparents. Then write a paragraph about your family using the tree and the texts above to help you.

....

....

....

....

....

....

....

....

3 **Word work:** positive and negative adjectives about people

Put the words and phrases in the correct column depending on whether you think they are mainly positive or mainly negative (some of these are a matter of opinion not fact).

| patient   strict   affectionate   kind   honest   wild   serious   happy |
| good sense of humor   a lot of fun   boring   sociable   wonderful   shy   dependable |
| violent   good company   funny   great   unhappy |

Positive		Negative	
....	....	....	....
....	....	....	....
....	....	....	....
....	....	....	....
....	....	....	....

4 **Skills work:** writing 2

Think of a favorite relative and write a paragraph describing him / her. Try to include some of their faults as well as the things you like about them. Use the words above if you want.

....

....

....

....

....

2 Partners

Language summary: describing people's physical appearance

Use:

- To talk about people's general appearance, use *to be* + adjective.
  She is tall. He's slim. I'm average height.
- To talk about their eyes or hair, use *to have* + adjective + noun.
  He has short hair. I have blue eyes.
  But: *My eyes are blue. His hair is short and straight.*

Form:

He / She	's (is)	tall. slim.	
His / Her	eyes	are	blue. green.
	hair	is	short. brown.
I	have	black hair.	
He / She	has	brown eyes.	

---

1 Language work

Complete the sentences using the correct form of *to be* or *to have*.

His eyes ......*are*...... brown and his hair ....*is*....... black.

1 She .... tall and slim and she .... green eyes.

2 My hair .... blond and my eyes .... blue.

3 I .... average height and I .... brown wavy hair.

4 He .... green eyes and his hair .... gray.

5 I .... long black hair and I .... short.

2 Skills work: reading and writing

a Read these eight advertisements and match each man with one of the women.

MAN 1

I'm a 30-year-old man and I'm tall and slim and my friends say I'm quite attractive. I like music and reading but I don't go out much. I want to meet someone who likes staying in with a good book or a nice video. Looks aren't important.

MAN 3

Tall, slim man seeks sociable woman aged 20–35. I'm very sociable with a good sense of humor but I'm afraid I'm not very attractive. However I enjoy going to restaurants and to the movies and compatibility is more important to me than looks.

MAN 2

Hi, I'm sure you'd love to meet me! I'm sociable and friendly and I love going to the beach on my motorcycle. I'm tall and seriously good looking with blue eyes and black hair. You have to be as good looking as me and like the same things.

MAN 4

Slim man (45) of average height with wavy brown hair and blue eyes likes good food and wine and traveling. I would like to meet a younger, smaller woman who likes evenings out and weekends away.

WOMAN A
Small, woman – a bit fat! – seeks funny man who likes going out and having fun. I enjoy eating out and going to movies and plays. Age, appearance, etc. unimportant.

WOMAN C
Very attractive tall slim woman, blue eyes, blond hair etc. wants really good-looking man to take her out and show her a good time. I enjoy all kinds of activities but especially going out dancing and being outdoors with the wind in my hair. Call me.

WOMAN B
Very shy woman likes books and movies but doesn't like going out except to concerts. Would like to meet slim, good-looking man for friendship maybe more. I can be very sociable with the right man!

WOMAN D
Short 32-year-old woman likes going out for candlelit dinners and romantic weekends in the mountains, is looking for an older man. Looks not as important as someone who is kind and wants to take care of me.

b Write a brief description of each of these people.

1 <u>She's small and slim. She has short brown hair and brown eyes.</u>

2 ....

3 ....

4 ....

5 ....

6 ....

3 Love and friendship

Language summary: using object pronouns after verbs and prepositions			
Use:	**Form:**		
Use object pronouns – *me, you, him, her, it, us, you, them* – after verbs and prepositions.	I		her.
	You	talked to	him.
*She looked at **him**.*	He	listened to	us.
*He gave **us** some lovely flowers.*	They		them.

1 Language work

a Complete the table with the correct prepositions – the first one is done for you.

Subject	**Possessive**	**Object**
I	my	me
....	....	....
....	....	....
....	....	....
....	....	....
....	....	....
....	....	....
....	....	....

b Correct the mistakes.

Me ....**my**.... boyfriend's name is José. He loves my .... and I love her .... Him .... sisters are named.............
Katrina and Lucia. We see their .... quite often and watch their .... playing on your .... bicycles. For your
.... birthday, José gave Katrina a kitten and she gave our .... a nice picture. The kitten is lovely and we all like playing
with it and watching its .... chasing your .... tail.

2 Word work: weddings

a Put the words in the correct column.

| bride   good luck   whale's tooth   candy   groom   jewelry   customs   handkerchiefs |
| horseshoe   gifts   coins   relatives   bride's father   purses |

People		Things / concepts	
bride		good luck	

b Now use a dictionary to help you add two or three words to each column.

3 Word work: describing people

Without looking back at this unit or at your Student's Book, try to fill in this spidergram. When you finish, check your answers in the Student's Book.

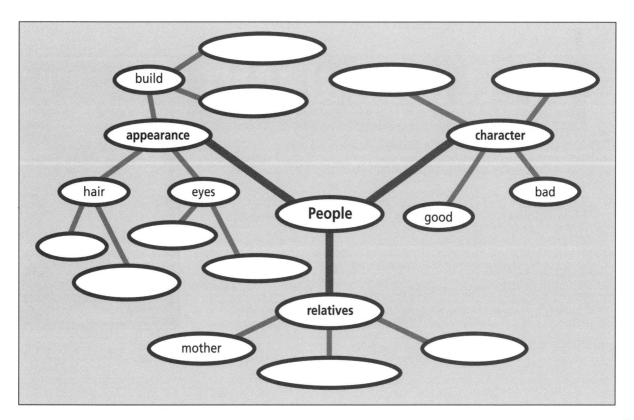

Unit 4 Work and play

1 Twenty-four hours

1 **Word work:** patterns of work

a Match these words / phrases about work with their definitions.

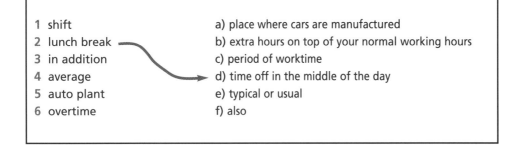

1 shift		a) place where cars are manufactured
2 lunch break		b) extra hours on top of your normal working hours
3 in addition		c) period of worktime
4 average		d) time off in the middle of the day
5 auto plant		e) typical or usual
6 overtime		f) also

b Fill in the blanks in this text with one of the words / phrases.

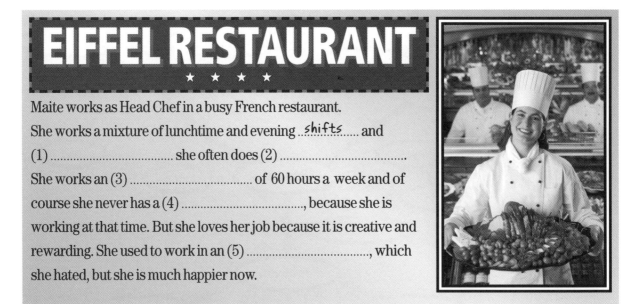

EIFFEL RESTAURANT
★ ★ ★ ★

Maite works as Head Chef in a busy French restaurant.
She works a mixture of lunchtime and evening ...shifts..... and
(1) .... she often does (2) ....
She works an (3) .... of 60 hours a week and of
course she never has a (4) ...., because she is
working at that time. But she loves her job because it is creative and
rewarding. She used to work in an (5) ...., which
she hated, but she is much happier now.

2 Skills work: reading

Read this letter from Maite to Pablo and then answer the questions.

April 10

Dear Pablo,

I thought I'd just send you a quick note and let you know how I'm doing. I'm enjoying my new job at the Eiffel very much and all the other staff are very friendly but I have to work really long hours. Some days I start at 10 in the morning and finish about 5 and other days I start at 5 and don't finish until about 2 in the morning. I also sometimes work overtime! I prefer the evening shift in some ways because it's more fun and lively. At least I don't have to take any work home with me – once I finish at 2 a.m., that's it! I don't really have a lunch or a dinner break but I do get some weekends off.

How about you? How's your job at the auto plant? Please say Hello to everyone for me. Do write and let me know how you're doing – or send me an e-mail!

Lots of love,

Maite

Are these statements true or false? Put T for true and F for false.

Maite and Pablo are friends. ....T....

1 They work together. ....

2 Maite hates her new job. ....

3 The other people who work in the restaurant are friendly. ....

4 Maite never works overtime. ....

5 She sometimes takes work home with her. ....

6 She prefers working in the daytime. ....

7 She works every weekend. ....

> **Language note**
>
> Use *a* with *day / week / month / year* to mean *per* or *every*.
> *I work 8 hours a day.*
> *She goes there once a week.*
> (not "one time")
> *We see them about twice a month.*
> (not "two times")
> *I go to the gym three times a week.*

3 Skills work: writing

Write 5 true sentences about yourself, using *a day, a week, a month*, etc.

....I eat three times a day...

1 ....

2 ....

3 ....

4 ....

5 ....

2 Work and gender

Language summary: talking about how often you do things					
Use:	**Form:**				
Use adverbs of frequency – *always, often, usually, sometimes, rarely, never*. Put the adverb of frequency before the verb **except** with the verb *to be*.	I We They	often sometimes	go	to the movies.	
subject + adverb + verb subject + *to be* + adverb	He She	never	goes		
*I **often** visit my sister.*	I	am	always usually	at home	on Sundays.
*We **never** watch videos.* *He is **usually** at home in the afternoon.*	She	is			

1 Language work

Write these sentences in the correct order.

Sometimes they movies to go the.

   They sometimes go to the movies.

1 Is she school often at.

   ....

2 Visit never they us.

   ....

3 Always and are friendly kind you.

   ....

4 Travel we abroad rarely.

   ....

5 The bus stops usually here.

   ....

2 Skills work: writing

Think of someone you know – a relative or friend – and answer these questions about him / her, using *sometimes, never, once / twice a week*, etc. Write complete sentences.

How often does he / she go to the theater?

   She goes once or twice a week.

1 Where is he / she usually in the mornings?

   ....

2 How often does he / she speak English?

   ....

3 How often does he / she go abroad?

   ....

4 How often is he / she out on the town?

....

5 How often does he / she ride the bus?

....

3 Skills work: reading

a **Put this conversation in the correct order by numbering the lines. The first one is done for you.**

.... **A:** What about sports – do you play sports?

.... **B:** Oh, very rarely. Maybe about twice a year but they need it more, I know.

.... **A:** Excuse me. I'm doing a survey about housework and leisure activities. Could I ask you a few questions?

.... **A:** How often do you clean the windows?

.... **B:** We sometimes play tennis and my husband goes to the gym but my favorite sport is playing video games.

.... **A:** Do you go out much?

.... **B:** Oh, about once a week on average, I guess, but my husband sometimes does it too.

.... **A:** Do you often clean the apartment?

.... **B:** Yes, sure, that's OK.

b **Now correct these mistakes about the conversation. Write complete sentences.**

The woman never plays tennis.

She sometimes plays tennis. ....

1 Her favorite sport is pool.

....

2 Her husband never cleans the apartment.

....

3 They clean the windows once a month.

....

4 The woman sometimes goes to the gym.

....

3 Vacations

1 Word work: national holidays

a Put these words / phrases in the correct column. Don't look at your Student's Book.

| picnics   colonies   parades   prisoners   Declaration of Independence   revolutionaries |
| celebrations   fireworks   national holiday   republic |

Independence Day	Bastille Day	Either
colonies	....	....
....	....	....
....	....	....
....	....	....

b Now look at the text in your Student's Book and read it again to check your answers.

Language summary: uses of the present progressive

Use:				Form:		
• Use the present progressive to talk about things which are happening now **(A)**: *I'm reading the newspaper.*				I	am	watching television.
				He She	is	visiting friends.
• to talk about things happening around now over a period of time **(B)**: *She's staying with her brother.*				We They	are	staying in Los Angeles. leaving tomorrow.
• to talk about future arrangements, usually involving other people **(C)**: *He's meeting her tomorrow.*						

2 Language work

a Correct the mistakes.

You walking in the street. ....*You're walking in the street.   (A)*...

1 We writing an exercise. ....

2 He are learning English at college. ....

3 She speaks to her mother on the phone at the moment.

....

4 I going away next weekend. ....

5 They is watching the ball game later. ....

b Now write A, B or C next to each of these sentences depending on which use of the present progressive it is (see the uses A, B and C in the Language summary). The example has been done for you.

3 Skills work: writing

Think of someone you know – a relative or friend – and write some sentences about their current activities and future arrangements.

....

....

....

....

....

4 Word work: crossword

Complete this crossword by answering the questions. The words are about work, leisure and celebrations. The number in parentheses represents the number of letters in the word.

¹F ²I N ³A N C ⁴I A L Y ⁵E A ⁶R

Across

1 Another way of saying fiscal year. (9,4)
7 Do you .... go abroad? (4)
8 Opposite of *always* (5)
10 Supporter of sudden and sometimes violent political change (13)
13 .... (every) one spoke at the meeting (4)
14 You don't say "......" times a day. You say "twice" (3)
15 *We are* is part of the verb *to* .... (2)
16 I get .... to work at 7 a.m. (2)
17 She works in .... office (2)
18 Yesterday I .... two kilometers (3)
19 .... is a male model (2)
20 Pleased to .... you! (4)
22 We like .... new apartment (3)
23 I / my; .... / our (2)
24 I think you .... the answer (4)

Down

2 July 4th is .... Day in the U.S.A. (12)
3 Close to (4)
4 After you wash your clothes sometimes you .... them (4)
5 I finish work at 3 .... (5,9)
6 Do you ever go to clubs? Yes but very .... (6)
9 Time off in the middle of the day (10)
11 Extra hours at work can be called .... (8)
12 How .... do you go to concerts? (5)
15 My job is to serve drinks. I work in a .... (3)
19 .... old are you? (3)
21 She was a student. What's she doing .... ? (3)

Unit 5 Time out

1 On the town

1 Skills work: reading

a Look at the photo.
Do you know where it is?
Do you know anything about it?

b Read the text and then
do exercises c and d.

c Look at these words from the text
and try to guess their meaning
from the context.

> arranged   thematically
> breathtaking   scale
> upper   overlooking

Now use a dictionary to check.

TATE MODERN

Tate Modern was opened in London in 2000 in a massive building which used to be a power station. It has a wonderful collection of paintings and sculptures which are arranged thematically, including works by Picasso, Monet, Andy Warhol and many many others. Some people go just to see the building, which has been beautifully converted and is quite breathtaking in its scale. It also has marvellous views of the Thames and St Paul's Cathedral, especially from the upper floors.

The museum has a restaurant, cafeteria and a terrace overlooking the river where you can have drinks on summer evenings.

Hours: Sunday to Thursday: 10 a.m.–6 p.m., Friday and Saturday: 10 a.m.–10 p.m.
ADMISSION: FREE

d Write full answers to these questions.

What is Tate Modern?

   .....Tate Modern is an art gallery..

1 Where is Tate Modern?

   ....

2 What is included in the collection?

   ....

3 What is special about the museum?

   ....

4 Where can you get a drink in the museum?

   ....

5 Which evenings is the museum open late?

   ....

6 How much is the admission fee?

   ....

Language summary: talking about location and directions

Use:

• Look at the way these prepositions are used to describe location:
on Southwark Street *at* the corner *behind* the movie theater *across from* St Paul's
between the theater *and* the station

• Remember to say *next to* the church but *near* the bookstore (without to).

• To give directions, use *Turn left, turn right, go three blocks, cross the street,
you're at the station. It's on your left / right.*

2 Word work: street directions

a Fill in the blanks in this text.

Tate Modern is .....**on**..... the South Bank

(1) .... St Paul's Cathedral. It is

(2) .... the Globe Theater and

Bankside Gallery. If you are coming from

Cannon Street station, (3) ....

on Upper Thames Street, (4) ....

two blocks, then (5) .... the river

(6) .... Southwark Bridge. (7) ....

on Bankside, walk along Bankside and the

museum is (8) .... left, (9) ....

Queen's Walk.

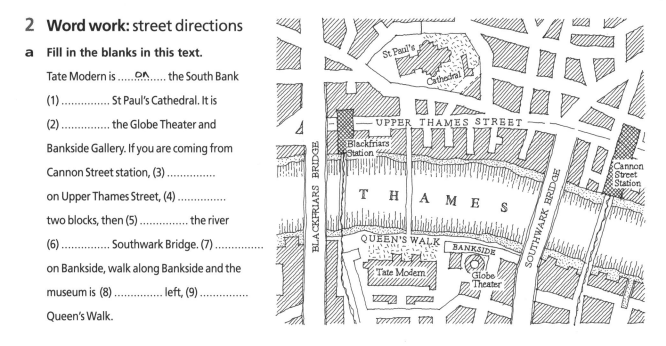

b Now complete these spidergrams with prepositions and nouns that go together.

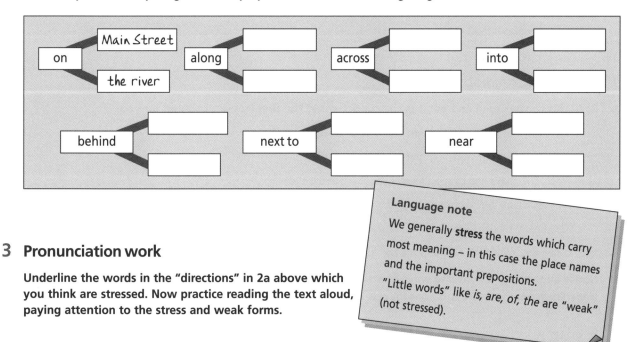

on — Main Street / the river

along

across

into

behind

next to

near

3 Pronunciation work

**Underline the words in the "directions" in 2a above which
you think are stressed. Now practice reading the text aloud,
paying attention to the stress and weak forms.**

Language note

We generally **stress** the words which carry
most meaning – in this case the place names
and the important prepositions.
"Little words" like *is, are, of, the* are "weak"
(not stressed).

2 What's on?

Language summary: talking about likes / wishes, making, accepting and rejecting suggestions

Use:

- Use the gerund (verb + *ing*) to talk about things you generally like / love / enjoy.
  *I **like reading**. I **love dancing**. I **enjoy going** to the movies.*
- With *like* and *love* you can also use the infinitive, but not with *enjoy*. *I **like to watch** movies. I **love to eat** out.*
- For specific wishes use *I'd like to (I would like to).*
  *I'd **like to eat** out tonight. I'd **prefer to visit** friends tomorrow.*
- For suggestions, use *Why don't we* or *Let's* + the infinitive without *to*. ***Why don't we go** to that new Chinese place?*
  ***Let's go** to a movie.*
- You can answer suggestions by accepting them:
  Good idea. That's fine with me.
  or rejecting them:
  I'd rather not. No, I don't think so, thanks.

Form:

I	like love	to go going	to the theater.
She	enjoys	seeing	movies.
Why don't we Let's		have dinner out tonight. eat out.	
I'd	like prefer	to stay home.	

---

1 Skills work: reading

a Read this conversation and put it in the correct order. The first line is numbered for you.

.... I'd prefer not to. I had Italian last night. What about Chinese?

.... I don't really enjoy watching sports. Let's go out to eat.

.... Yeah, OK, that's fine by me. I'll meet you there at 8 o'clock.

...1... Hi, would you like to go out tonight?

.... OK, fine. Why don't we go to that new Italian restaurant?

.... Yeah, OK. Why don't we go to the ball game?

b Notice all the suggestions and ways of accepting / rejecting them in the conversation.
Underline them. The first one is done for you.

c Correct the mistakes in this conversation.

A: Hello, how are you doing?

B: Fine, thanks.

A: Would you like going out tonight?

 Would you like to go out tonight? ....

B: Good idea. Why don't we going to the theater?

 ....

A: No, I don't think so. I'm a bit too tired for that. Let's just to go out for a drink.

 ....

B: Fine with me. Do you like drink outside?

 ....

A: Oh, yes, good idea. Let's to go to the bar on the river.

 ....

2 Skills work: writing

a What would you say in these situations?

Friend: Hey! Let's go to the new jazz bar.

(Imagine you think jazz is boring. Give your opinion and suggest another place.)

 ...... _I don't like jazz. How about going to a salsa club instead?_ ....

1 A person you meet at a party: What do you like doing on weekends?

 (List the things you like.) ....

2 A friend: Would you prefer to go the movies or a restaurant?

 (Imagine you went to the movies last night.) ....

3 A colleague at work: Why don't we go to a fish restaurant?

 (Imagine you never eat fish.) ....

4 A friend: What would you like to do this weekend?

 (Suggest some ideas.) ....

5 A friend: Did you hear? Jane's in the hospital!

 (Suggest an idea.) ....

3 Party time

Language summary: talking about definite plans and predictions and making offers

Use:

• Use *to be* + *going to* to talk about definite plans or intentions.
  *I'm **going to** have a party next week.*
  *He's **going to** cook dinner.*
• Use *will* to say what you think will happen:
  You'll like the movie. It's really good.
  and to make offers:
  I'll make the salad. I'll get the tickets.

Form:

I'm		
He's	going to	have a party.
They're		
You'll	enjoy it.	
I'll	make the sandwiches.	

---

1 Language work

Complete this conversation, using the correct form of *will* or *going to*.

A: I'm going to have a party next Saturday. Would you like to come?

B: I'd love to but I (1) .... cook dinner for my parents on Saturday.

A: Can't you change it? I think it (2) .... be a great party.

There (3) .... be lots of people there that you (4) .... like.

B: Well, OK, I guess so, but I don't think they (5) .... be very happy.

A: I'm sure it (6) .... be OK.

B: All right. Fine. I (7) .... make a dessert.

A: I don't really have any dance music.

B: OK, I (8) .... bring some.

A: Great!

2 **Skills work:** writing

a **Write five true sentences about yourself, using** *going to.*

This afternoon *I'm going to leave work at 5.00 p.m.* ....

1 Tonight ....

2 Tomorrow ....

3 Next weekend ....

4 Next month ....

5 Next year ....

b **Make some predictions about the general future, using** *will.* **Complete the sentences.**

When I get home tonight *it'll be dark.* ....

1 I think tomorrow the weather ....

2 After I finish this course, I think ....

3 In the next few years, people ....

4 By 2050, the world ....

5 In the next few months, my family ....

3 **Word work:** entertainment

Without looking in your Student's Book, try to put these words in the correct column.

dip   museum   across   admission fee   sodas   stereo   opening hours   right   peanuts telling jokes   behind   gallery   exhibits   blocks   charades   next to   potato chips sculpture   between   near   CDs   collection   lemonade   turn left

Location / direction	Entertainment	Parties
across	admission fee	dip

Unit 6 In the past

1 Personal history

1 Language work

Write the past simple of these verbs.

love   loved...........................

1 establish	....	**5** travel	....
2 marry	....	**6** enjoy	....
3 hate	....	**7** move	....
4 live	....	**8** compete	....

2 Skills work: reading and writing

a Read these notes about Courtney Pine and look back at the article in your Student's Book about Christopher Reeve. Using the notes and the article to help you, write a paragraph about Courtney Pine's life.

At a family wedding, aged 5

Courtney Fitzgerald Pine
Born: March 18 1964, London.
Education: William Wilberforce primary school, London; Rutherford school; Kingsbury high school.

Married: 1995 June Guishard (one son: Jemaal, 14; five daughters:

Cool school, aged 19

Cleopatra and Shona – deceased; Isis, 7; Jenae, 5; Taiyo, 3.

Albums: Journey To The Urge Within, 1986; Destiny's Song, 1988; The Vision's Tale, 1989; Closer To Home, 1990; Within The Realms Of Our Dreams, 1991; To The Eyes Of Creation, 1992; Modern Day Jazz

With the Jazz Warriors, aged 24

Stories, 1996; Underground, 1997; Another Story (remix), 1998; Back In The Day, 2000.

Awards: 1996 Mercury music prize nomination; 1996 and 1997 MOBO for best jazz act; 1999 People's Choice best British jazz act for blues and soul; 2000 OBE.

b Now write a similar paragraph about yourself.

....

....

....

....

....

....

3 Pronunciation work

a Look at these words from previous units and underline the stressed syllable.
The first one has been done for you.

| engin<u>eer</u>   questionnaire   thirty   cafeteria   fairly   purses   birthday   parents   serious |

b Now put the words in the correct column, depending on the sound of the stressed syllable.

aire	eer	ir
questionnaire	....	....
....	....	....
....		....

c Now put words from exercise 3a into this conversation.

A: Excuse me, I'm filling out a ...questionnaire...
Could you answer some questions, please?

B: Sure.

A: OK, first question. How old are you?

B: (1) .... It was my

(2) .... yesterday!

A: Really! Congratulations. And what do you do?

B: I'm an (3) ....

A: Good. OK, and the last question. What do your parents do, please?

B: They run a (4) .... It's hard work, but the money is (5) .... good!

Unit 6 Lesson 2

2 Growing up

> **Language summary:** the past simple of irregular verbs
>
> **Use:**
> • The past simple forms of irregular verbs are all different but most of them are quite similar to the infinitive form.
> *come / came see / saw meet / met write / wrote fall / fell*
> • You can really only learn irregular past simple forms by memorizing them. But you can help yourself by thinking of ways to remember them, e.g. by thinking of a simple sentence with a similar sound or rhyme:
> *I took the book*
> or by grouping them in your mind:
> *hit put set   taught caught bought*

1 Language work

a Look at these infinitive forms. Put the past simple form in the correct column, depending on whether it is regular or irregular.

> love   give   take   work   graduate   hear   hit   make   act   get   leave
> establish   read   grow   fly   say   be   win   spend   do   want   buy
> begin   like   live   meet   become

Regular		Irregular			
loved		gave			

b Look at the back of your Student's Book and check your answers.

36

c Write these sentences in the past simple.

Every day I go to class. .... Yesterday I went to class. ....

1 We are writing an exercise. ....

2 Every week we take our sister to basketball. ....

3 Every week he writes to his grandmother. ....

4 Every month I read several books. ....

5 Every month she buys some new clothes. ....

6 Every year they fly to Europe. ....

7 Every year they spend lots of money. ....

d Now write four true sentences about yourself, using the past simple.

1 Yesterday I ....

2 Last week I ....

3 Last month I ....

4 Last year I ....

2 Skills work: reading and writing

a Read the article in your Student's Book about Jenny Ford again and look at your completed chart about her.

b Now fill in this chart for yourself.

Name	Favorite subjects	Ambition(s)	Taste in music	First love
....	....	....	....	....
....	....	....	....	....

c Use your chart to write a paragraph about your high school days.

....

....

....

....

....

Unit 6 Lesson 3

3 Crime stories

> **Language note**
> Use *steal* with the thing taken and *rob* with the person or place it is taken from.
> They **stole** a lot of money. They **robbed** the old man.

1 Word work: *rob* and *steal*

Use the correct form of *rob* or *steal* to complete these sentences.

She ..*steals*.. from the rich to give to the poor.

1 Yesterday a gang .... the Chase Manhattan Bank.

2 They .... a huge amount of money.

3 Some girls .... the old lady last week.

4 Every week he .... several cars and sells them.

5 It is common for gangs to .... tourists.

2 Skills work: reading

Read this article about a bank robbery.

On October 13, 1969 a gang of masked thieves robbed a small branch of the Washington Bank. When they first walked into the bank, a woman <u>was standing</u> at the counter and a clerk was serving her. The bank manager was sitting at his desk, talking on the phone. The robbers pulled out guns and made everyone lie on the floor. They opened the cash register and took all the money, then immediately ran out of the bank and jumped into their car, which was waiting outside for them. When the police arrived, everyone was still lying on the floor, absolutely terrified.

Are these statements true or false? Write T for true and F for false.

The thieves were wearing masks. ..T..

1 They ran into the bank.	....	4 The thieves stole the money from the safe.	....
2 A clerk was serving a man.	....	5 They escaped in a van.	....
3 The bank manager was making a phone call.	....	6 When the police came there was no one in the bank.	....

Language summary: past progressive

Use:

• Use the past progressive to talk about actions in the past which were in progress at a specific time:
*At 7:30 they **were having** their dinner.*

• or when something else happened: *They **were having** dinner when their friends arrived.*

Form:

I He	was	walking down the street	when	I he	saw	an old friend.
They	were			they		

---

3 Language work

a Look back at the text about the bank robbery and underline all the examples of the past progressive. Think about why it is used in each case.
The first example is underlined for you.

b Correct the mistakes in this story.

Last night a young man walked along Main Street when two teenage girls were jumping out from behind a tree and attacked him. They were taking his wallet and his watch. The man was starting to scream. Two boys were hearing him and they came running to help. When they were reaching him, the girls already ran away.

---

4 Word work: word search

Look for verbs in the past simple and words and phrases about school and crime in this word search. Then write them in the correct column. You can go across or down and you can use the same letter twice.

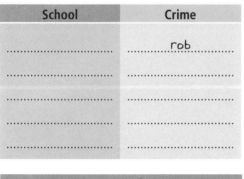

School	Crime
....	.... rob ....
....	....
....	....
....	....
....	....

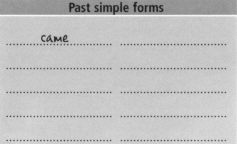

Past simple forms	
.... came	....
....	....
....	....
....	....
....	

E	S	C	A	P	E	D	R	O	B
C	T	A	G	A	N	R	E	H	I
O	E	M	A	Y	G	A	A	I	O
N	A	E	N	R	L	W	D	S	L
M	L	A	G	O	I	I	S	T	O
I	A	P	A	L	S	N	O	O	G
C	S	U	O	L	H	G	S	R	Y
S	A	T	F	L	E	W	A	Y	O
A	F	O	U	G	H	T	I	L	L
W	E	N	T	H	I	T	D	I	D

Unit 7 Learning for life

1 School days

1 Word work: subjects and specialists

Language note

You can add an ending to many school / college subjects to form the word for someone who specializes in that subject.

math – mathematician
biology – biologist
geography – geographer

Look at these school / college subjects. Change the word for the subject into the word for the person: *economics* ⟶ *economist*. Put the new word into the correct column. Use a dictionary to help you.

| economics science history journalism chemistry interpreting languages art |
| physics photography agriculture botany astronomy plumbing |

-ist	-ian	-er
economist		

2 Pronunciation work

Underline the stressed syllable in the words in the box and in the specialist words in your table.
Use a dictionary to help you.
Two examples have been done for you.

Language note

Stress often stays the same but sometimes changes:
bi<u>o</u>logy – bi<u>o</u>logist
ge<u>o</u>graphy – ge<u>o</u>grapher but
<u>his</u>tory – his<u>to</u>rian

3 Word work: specialists

a Choose five of the specialist words you think would be useful for you to remember and write definitions like this.

A scientist is someone who studies or works in the field of science.

1 ....

2 ....

3 ....

4 ....

5 ....

b Match these words / phrases with their definitions.

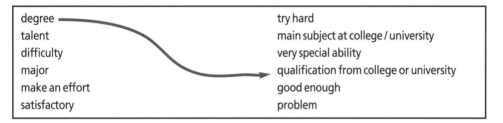

degree	try hard
talent	main subject at college / university
difficulty	very special ability
major	qualification from college or university
make an effort	good enough
satisfactory	problem

4 Skills work: writing

a Look again at the school reports in your Student's Book and the paragraphs about Jennifer and Anita.

b Read this report of another student, Juan, and then write a paragraph about him.

BARNDALE HIGH SCHOOL – REPORT

Student: Juan Jimenez

Subject	Grade	Comments
Math	A	Excellent
History	B	Good work
English	B+	Good work
Physics	A	Excellent
Physical education	C	Could make a better effort
French	B	Did good work this year
Computer science	A	Excellent
Geography	A	Excellent

....

....

....

....

....

....

....

....

....

2 Choices

1 Skills work: reading

a Read this article quickly once. What do you think a year off is? Write the answer here.

....

TAKING A YEAR OFF

In many countries nowadays it is very common for kids to take a year off. This is a great idea, especially if you are not sure what subject you want to study at college or what field of work you want to end up in. It gives you more time to think about it.

There are several options for what to do during your year off. Many young people go backpacking while others gain valuable work experience doing volunteer work or helping with a charity. One disadvantage of taking a year off is that it can be quite expensive. It also delays the time when you get your degree and when you can start earning a salary. But for most people, the advantages are greater than the disadvantages. Taking a year off builds character and the experience you gain is something that will always look impressive on your resume.

b What do you think these words mean? Try to guess from the context or from words which may be similar in your own language.
Write a definition or explanation next to each word.

option...*thing you can choose*................................ backpacking ....

charity .... salary ....

advantage.. gain ....

impressive .... resume ....

c Now read the article again and make notes under these headings:

Options for your year off	Advantages	Disdvantages
volunteer work	builds character	expensive
....	....	....
....	....	....

Language summary: comparing two things or people

Use:	Form:

Use:	Form:					
• Use a comparative adjective to compare two things or people and *than* (not *that*) to join the two ideas. *John is **smaller than** Caroline.* *Canada is **colder than** New Zealand.*	This one	is	nicer	than	that one.	
	These	are	easier		those.	
• For short adjectives add *-er*: *smaller colder*			bigger			
• and double the consonant if it is a one-syllable adjective with a single vowel and ending in a consonant: *big – bigger slim – slimmer*			smaller more interesting more expensive better			
• For long adjectives (two syllables or more) use *more* + adjective: ***more** expensive **more** beautiful*			worse			
• For two-syllable adjectives ending in *-y* change the *y* to *i* and add *-er*: *prettier sillier*						

> **Language note**
> The comparative forms of *good* and *bad* are irregular:
> *better   worse*

2 Language work

a Complete the table.

Adjective	Comparative form		Adjective	Comparative form	
cheap	cheaper	than	5 intelligent	....	than
1 young	....	than	6 famous	....	than
2 modern	....	than	7 thin	....	than
3 happy	....	than	8 dirty	....	than
4 exclusive	....	than	9 extreme	....	than

b Write these sentences again, correcting the mistakes.

My brother is 7 years more old that me. Although I am more young that him, I am intelligenter and handsomer.

I am more tall and slimer than he is and one day, when I am a bit biger, I will be a lot famouser.

....

....

....

3 Skills work: writing

Look again at your notes on taking a year off and finish writing this paragraph about the advantages and disadvantages, using comparative adjectives. Use the ideas from the text and add some ideas of your own.

Taking a year off can be a lot more expensive than going straight to college but it can also be a lot ...

....

....

....

....

....

3 Learning culture

Language summary: *can / could / would*			
Use:	**Form:**		

Use:
- Use *can you* (informal) and *could you* (formal) to ask other people to do things.
  Can you open the window?
  Could you lend me some money, please?
- Use *could I* + infinitive or *would you mind if I* + present simple or past simple to ask for permission:
  Could I speak to you for a moment?
  Would you mind if I use / used your phone?
- Both of these are quite formal or polite.

Form:

Can Could	you	open the window close the door help me with this	please?
Would you mind if I		use used	your phone?

1 Language work

a Write these requests in the correct order.

Window open you please could?

Could you open the window, please?

1 early you leave I mind if would?

....

2 for carry me you this please can?

....

3 me call you could later?

....

4 tomorrow finished mind you if would I this?

....

5 me ride you give could please a?

....

b **Write requests / ask for permission for the following situations:**

You are lost. Ask for directions.
Could you tell me how to get to the station, please?

1 You need a pen. Ask your best friend.

2 You need next Friday off. Ask your boss politely.

3 It is very hot in the room. Ask your colleague politely to open the window.

4 You need to leave class early. Ask your teacher very politely.

5 You want a cup of coffee. Ask your sister to make you one.

c **Write requests using comparative adjectives.**

This belt is too short. *Could you find me a longer one?*

1 This shirt is too small. Could you . . . . ?

2 This coffee is cold. . . . . ?

3 This train is too slow. . . . . ?

4 This exercise is really difficult. . . . . ?

5 I can't leave that late, I'm afraid. . . . . ?

d **Now match the sentences above with the people speaking in each one.**
An example has been done for you.

1 employee to boss   ....5....   3 student to teacher   ....   5 customer to waiter   ....

2 customer to clerk in store .... 4 passenger to booking clerk ....

2 Word work: nouns and verbs that go together

Notice how the nouns in the box can only go with only one or two of the verbs below: *study history win a scholarship.*

Look at these nouns about education / life experience and put them in the correct column depending on which verb they go with. If you think there is more than one possibility, put the noun in more than one column.

sociology an effort research high school volunteer work talent difficulty a good report
an interview a year off charity work college ability economics a request
a business course electrical engineering a vocational course a good grade
a state university architecture a research institute computer science

make	do	have	attend	study	take	get
				sociology		

45

Unit 8 On the move

1 Getting around

1 Word work: transportation

a Look at this table. Put a check (✓) for the characteristics which apply to each form of transportation. The first one has been done for you.

	wheels	with wings	with an engine	for more than 4 people
airplane	✓	✓	✓	✓
train	○	○	○	○
bicycle	○	○	○	○
automobile	○	○	○	○
horse	○	○	○	○
ferry	○	○	○	○

b Fill in the blanks with a suitable form of transportation. Try to use a different one each time.

A ..train.. has more wheels than an ..airplane..

1 A .... is faster than a ....

2 .... are generally more comfortable than ....

3 It is cheaper to travel by .... than by ....

4 .... carry more people than ....

5 A .... is cleaner than a ...., but it isn't as comfortable.

> **Language note**
> • *By* is used to say who did an action: *It was invented **by** George Stephenson.*
> • Also use *by* with transportation: *We went **by** bus.*

2 Word work: *by*

Fill in the spidergram with suitable words.

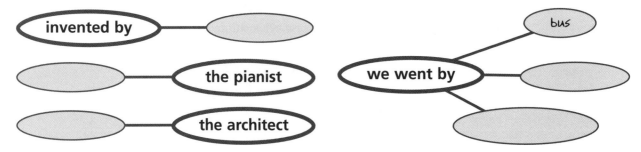

3 Skills work: reading

a Read this text about Eurostar and then do the exercises.

EUROSTAR

"THE FASTEST PASSENGER TRAIN IN THE WORLD"

One of the fastest and most modern passenger trains in the world is the Eurostar, which covers the distance between London and Paris in just three hours – a journey which used to take five or six hours and always involved a slow ferry crossing. You can leave London Waterloo at 4 o'clock on a Friday afternoon and be in the center of Paris in time for dinner.

One of the most exciting things about the Eurostar is that it goes through a tunnel under the sea. This part of the journey takes about 20 minutes and you don't really notice what is happening, but some people choose not to travel by the Eurostar because they find the idea quite frightening. The trains are very comfortable and there is a good variety of food and drink available in the buffet car.

One slight disappointment, though, is that the train travels so fast, particularly on the French side where it speeds up considerably, that you can't really see anything out of the window.

b What do you think these words mean? Try to guess from the context or from similar words in your own language. Write a definition or explanation next to the words.

ferry crossing ....

frightening ....

buffet car ....

slight ....

disappointment ....

speeds up ....

Now use a dictionary to check your guesses.

c Are these statements true or false? Put a check (✓) in the right circle.

You can get from Paris to London in one and a half hours.   T ◯   F ✓

1 The journey from London to Paris by train is much faster than it was.   T ◯   F ◯

2 You cross the sea by ferry on the Eurostar.   T ◯   F ◯

3 Some people are too scared to travel on the Eurostar.   T ◯   F ◯

4 You can buy drinks but no food on the train.   T ◯   F ◯

5 The train travels faster in France than it does in England.   T ◯   F ◯

2 Getting away from it all

Language summary: comparing three or more people or things

Use:	Form:			
• Use superlative adjectives to say which of three or more people / things is the biggest, best, etc. *It's **the prettiest** hotel in town.* *She's **the oldest** woman in the world.* • Look back at the rules for long and short adjectives when making comparative forms and for spelling. The rules for superlatives are the same, but don't forget to use *the* adjective + *-est* or *the most* + adjective (not *the more*!): *the **longest** river the **most expensive** car*	It's	the highest	mountain	in the world.
		the longest	river	
		the smallest	country	
		the most expensive	diamond	
		the most beautiful	picture	

Language note
The superlative forms of *good* and *bad* are irregular:
the best restaurant   *the worst* food

1 Language work

a Look back at the article about the Eurostar on the previous page and underline the examples of the superlative form.
("One of <u>the fastest</u> ...")
Think about why it is used in each case.

b Some of these sentences are correct and some are not.
Put a check (✓) next to the correct sentences and write a correct sentence next to the others.

She is the most fast runner on the track.   ◯   *She is the fastest runner on the track.* ....

1 He is the more intelligent boy in the class.   ◯   ....

2 It is the longest river in the world.   ◯   ....

3 They are my best friends.   ◯   ....

4 That is the worse book I've ever read.   ◯   ....

5 It is one of most exclusive hotels in the world.   ◯   ....

C Fill in the blanks in this text using the superlative form of the adjective in parentheses. Don't forget to use *the*.

Madrid – the capital and (big) .....the biggest..... city in Spain.

It is one of (hot) .... places in the summer and sometimes

(cold) .... in the winter but always with

(exciting) .... nightlife.

Barcelona – probably (cosmopolitan) .... city

with (interesting) .... collection of art and

architecture in the country. Also famous for some of

(good) .... food.

San Sebastián – perhaps (beautiful) .... city in

Spain, certainly on the north coast. In the Basque country, one of

(rich) .... areas in the country but also one

of (expensive) ....

Granada – historically one of (important) .... cities.

Famous for the Alhambra, one of (well-preserved) ....

examples of Islamic architecture in western Europe.

2 Skills work: writing

The following are answers to quiz questions about the world. Write suitable questions using superlative forms.

Asia. What is the biggest continent? ....

1 Everest ....

2 The Pacific ....

3 English ....

4 The Nile ....

5 Venus ....

6 Mexico City ....

3 Word work: hotels

Look at these jumbled letters for words / phrases about hotels.
Try to figure out what each word is.

tevalore ....elevator..........   3 tnfseis ntcree ....

1 glsnie ormo ....   4 trursteana ....

2 nnitse rcuot ....   5 niwgmism olpo ....

3 Getting there

Language summary: agreeing						
Use:		**Form:**				
Auxiliary verb + *too* and *so* + auxiliary verb (affirmative) when you agree *I love this hotel. – I do too.* *I like this city. – So do I.*		I	like	this music.	I		do	too.
				orange juice	So			I.

1 Language work

Write suitable responses for these statements.

He gets up late. ....*She does too.*......... 　　3 I speak another language. ....

1 I like learning English. .... 　　4 I'm hungry. ....

2 I can play guitar. .... 　　5 I can drive. ....

2 Skills work: writing

Look at this completed landing card and use the information to write a paragraph about Guillermo Martinez.

LANDING CARD

Welcome to the U.S.A.

1 Last name ... Martinez

2 First (given) name ... Guillermo

3 Date of birth ... 12 / 08 / 70

4 Flight no. ... AA 3751

5 Number of family members traveling with you ... None

6 Country of citizenship ... Colombia

7 Address in the US ... 61 East 53rd street# Apt.C, New York

8 Purpose of visit ... to see relatives

Guillermo Martinez is ....

....

....

....

....

3 Word work: traveling

a Put the words / phrases in the right place on the spidergram.

agricultural products   double room   well-preserved   delays   cosmopolitan   overbooking
landing card   carriage   squash court   facilities   nightlife
buffet car   mechanical problems   purpose of visit   ferry crossing

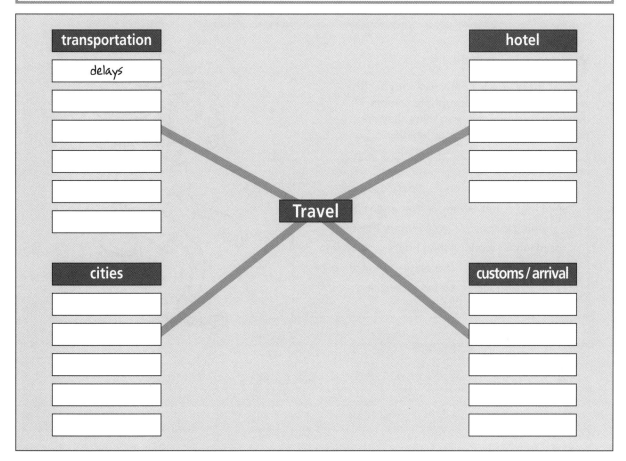

transportation
- delays

hotel

Travel

cities

customs / arrival

b Now add two words / phrases of your own under each heading.

c Use words from the spidergram in 3a to complete this text.

Dear Anna,

How's life? We're having a marvelous time here. Apart from a three-hour ....delay.......... before we left

Paris, it's been a perfect vacation! We booked a (1) .... in a five-star hotel on the beach. Great

(2) .... – squash courts, a fitness center and a swimming pool with a bar in the middle of it.

The food's good too and the (3) .... is unbelievable – dozens of night clubs and bars!

But tomorrow we're going to take a (4) .... to the island of Janboreen to see some wildlife. And

on Saturday we're going to visit the old part of the city which is very (5) ....

Say hi to Kevin!

Love, Lucy

Unit 9 Healthy living

1 Laughter is the best medicine

1 Word work: lifestyle

a Look at these words / phrases about health and put them in the appropriate column, depending on whether you think they are positive or negative for your health.

> junk food   fun   plenty of sleep
> smoking   relaxation   fruit and vegetables
> doing exercise   a sedentary lifestyle
> drinking   working long hours   bicycling
> cookies   stress   chocolate   watching TV
> fast food   coffee   walking

Positive		Negative		
plenty of sleep		junk food		

b Now add 3 words / phrases of your own to each column.

c Complete this text with words or phrases from exercise 1a.

Me? Unhealthy? No way! OK, I have a very ..*sedentary lifestyle*.. because I work 10 hours a day in front of a computer. I worry about my diet too! I eat a lot of (1) .... – hamburgers, cookies and cola. I also drink too much (2) .... , about seven cups a day! But I don't smoke! When I get home I enjoy relaxing, you know – (3) .... and listening to music. And (4) .... ? You mean bicycling, jogging and playing tennis? Not me! But let's be positive – I get (5) .... – eight hours a night. And am I worried about a heart attack? Well ... .

2 Skills work: reading

a Read this article about going to the gym. What does the writer think is strange about going to the gym?

Going to the gym

It is becoming increasingly popular nowadays for young people to spend part of their leisure time working out at the gym. Some people pay very high membership fees, then try to make sure of getting their money's worth by going to the gym at least three times a week. In some ways, this is a reaction to an otherwise sedentary lifestyle, which means that most young people spend several hours a day in front of a TV or computer screen.

They feel they need to balance this with vigorous exercise, especially if they are figure-conscious. It is also seen as "trendy" to dress up in the latest workout gear and go to the gym. Many parents feel nervous about letting their kids play or exercise in the street or in the park and the gym seems to offer a certain amount of safety. It does seem ironic, though, that people are willing to spend money to use machines which imitate things like walking, rowing and cycling when they could do the real thing in the fresh air and for free!

....
....

b Look at these words / phrases from the article. Try to guess what they mean from the context or from similar words / phrases in your own language.

> to work out   to get your money's worth   vigorous exercise   figure-conscious
>
> trendy   workout gear   ironic   willing   rowing

c Now use a dictionary to check your guesses.

d Now read the article again and make notes under these headings.

Going to the gym: Advantages	Going to the gym: Disadvantages
....	....
....	....
....	....
....	....

Unit 9 Lesson 2

2 Your favorite team

1 Word work: kinds of sports

Look at these words for sports / exercise and put a check (✓) in the boxes for the characteristics which apply to each one.

	riding	jogging	basketball	tennis	rugby
team	○	○	○	○	○
solo	✓	○	○	○	○
with a ball	○	○	○	○	○
with a racket	○	○	○	○	○
inside	○	○	○	○	○
outside	✓	○	○	○	○

Language summary: possessive pronouns

Use:			Form:		
Remember to use a possessive pronoun to avoid repeating the noun. *Is this her pen? No, it's **mine**.* (not *my pen*) *Is this your car? No, it's **his**.* (not *his car*).			Is this	your his her	car? book? pen?
			No, it isn't.	It's	theirs. hers. mine. his.

---

2 Language work

a Complete the table – some of this is review.

Subject	Object pronoun	Possesive adjective	Possesive pronoun
I	me	my	mine
you			
he			
she			
it			
we			
you			
they			

54

b Correct the mistakes.

Their team is more successful than our. ....~~than ours.~~..........

1 This isn't hers bicycle. It's my. ....

2 Yours brother looks like their. ....

3 My house is bigger than your. ....

4 Is this your hat? No, it's her. ....

5 I like theirs car more than mine. ....

3 Word work: spectator sport

a Match one of the words on the left with a definition on the right.

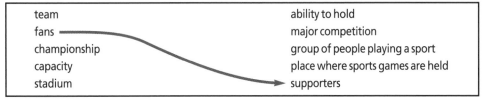

team	ability to hold
fans	major competition
championship	group of people playing a sport
capacity	place where sports games are held
stadium	supporters

b How much can you remember about Manchester United? Complete this text with words from exercise 3a.

Manchester United is one of the richest (1) .... clubs in the world. It is also one of the

best. The club has a long history and it won its first (2) .... in 1907. Old Trafford, its (3)

.... has a massive capacity and almost 70,000 (4) ....

go to watch their (5) .... when they play at home.

4 Skills work: writing

Look at the article in your Student's Book about Manchester United.
Use the article and the "vital statistics" to help you to write a paragraph about a sports team
in your country.

....
....
....
....
....
....

3 Open wide

Language summary: giving advice			
Use:	**Form:**		
You can use *you should, you need to* or *you have to* to give advice. *You have to* is the strongest and *you should* is the least strong. ~~You **should** see a doctor.~~ You **need to** go to the dentist every 6 months to keep your teeth healthy. You **have to** take care of your health.	You He She	should	go to the dentist every six months.
	You ~~She~~	need to ~~needs to~~	do some exercise. ~~eat less.~~
	He You	has to have to	stop smoking after that heart attack.

1 Language work

a Match these problems with a suitable piece of advice.

1 My gums bleed when I brush my teeth.   You have to take it easy.
2 I get lots of headaches.   You should floss every day.
3 My breath smells.   You need to go on a diet.
4 I'm a little overweight.   You should give up coffee.
5 I'm always tired.   You should use a mouthwash.

b Now write a suitable piece of advice for each of these problems.

I don't like my looks.
You shouldn't worry about them.

1 I spend hours in front of a computer every day.

2 I don't know what to do during vacations.

3 I like English but when I try to speak I feel shy.

4 My job is really stressful.

5 I often arrive late at work.

2 Pronunciation work

a Underline the stressed syllable on these words about sports and fitness.

<u>fill</u>ing   diet   windsurfing   overweight   toothbrush   mouthwash   cavity   karate

basketball   rugby   hiking   championship   stadium   sedentary habits

lifestyle   exercise   aerobics   referee

b Now say them aloud.

c Now put these words in the correct column depending on whether the "i"
sound is /i:/ (as in "feet") or /I/ (as in "sit").

tennis   jogging
teeth   visit
aerobics   team
dentist   cookies
screen   coffee

feet	sit
....	....
....	....
....	....
....	....
....	....

3 Word work: healthy living

a Put words from 2a and 2c in an appropriate place on the spidergram. You may
not find 7 for each catergory

dentist   exercise

filling

Health

soccer   good for you   bad for you

b Add two words of your own to each section.

Unit 10 The story so far

1 Turning points

1 Skills work: reading

a Read this article about Derek Walcott and answer the questions.

DEREK WALCOTT – *1992 Nobel Prize Literature Winner*

Derek Walcott is a very well-known writer. He has written several plays and many poems and has won a number of awards including, in 1992, the Nobel Prize for Literature.

Life has not always been easy for Derek, however. He was born in 1930 in St Lucia and raised in a poor family.

He went to St Mary's College in St Lucia and, later, to the University of the West Indies in Jamaica. He has worked as a schoolteacher and as a university lecturer at such prestigious institutions as Yale, Harvard and Columbia, as well as being a prolific writer.

His personal life has, unfortunately, not been as successful as his professional life. In 1954 he married Fay Moston but they were divorced in 1962, and he has since been married and divorced twice more. He had a son with Fay Moston and two daughters with his second wife, Margaret Maillard.

When was Derek Walcott born?

He was born in 1930.

....

1 Where was he educated?

....

2 What is he famous for?

....

3 Where has he worked?

....

4 How many times has he been married and divorced?

....

5 How many children does he have?

....

b **Try to think of another word or phrase for the following.**

well-known . . . .   awards . . . .   raised . . . .

lecturer . . . .   prestigious . . . .   prolific . . . .

c **Now use a dictionary to check your answers.**

2 Skills work: writing

Read the article about Derek Walcott again and write a similar account of someone you know, or of the person in the pictures. Use the text to help you.

. . . .

. . . .

. . . .

. . . .

. . . .

. . . .

. . . .

. . . .

. . . .

. . . .

2 Experience and experiences

Language summary: talking about past experiences			
Use:	**Form:**		
• Use the present perfect simple (*has / have* + past participle) to talk about your past experiences, especially if you don't say when they happened. *I've written several poems.*	I We They	have	written a book. been to India.
	He She	has	seen that movie.
• Use the same tense to talk about things which started in the past and still continue. *He's always worked here.*	I We	saw that movie in 1995. went to Brazil last summer.	
• Remember to use the past simple to talk about past experiences if you do specify when they happened. *She started college in 1987.*			

1 Language work 1

a Without looking back at the article about Derek Walcott, try to complete these statements about him, using either the present perfect or the past simple.

He ....*was born*........ in St Lucia in 1930.

1 After leaving school, he .... to college.

2 He .... several plays and many poems.

3 He .... a number of awards.

4 He .... the Nobel Prize for Literature in 1992.

5 He .... Fay Moston in 1954.

6 They .... in 1962.

b Now look back at the article to check your answers.
Think about why either the present perfect or the past simple is used in each case.

c Sort these irregular verb forms into their principal parts (infinitive form, past simple and past participle) in alphabetical order. Try to do this quickly!

go	swim	drank	knew	known	be	read	seen	had	read	been	gone
went	did	drink	read	see	do	saw	swum	have	written	know	
was	won	had	break	wrote	win	write	made	broken	make	fell	won
broke	came	fallen	made	done	fall	swam	come	drunk	come		

Infinitive	Past simple	Past participle	Infinitive	Past simple	Past participle
....	....	....	....	....	....
....	....	....	....	....	....
....	....	....	....	....	....

Infinitive	Past simple	Past participle	Infinitive	Past simple	Past participle
....	....	....	....	....	....
....	....	....	....	....	....
....	....	....	....	....	....
....	....	....	....	....	....
....	....	....	....	....	....

2 Language work 2

**Complete these sentences with
been / gone + to + the correct
form of have.**

.... _Has_ .... he ever .... _been_ .... to Rome?

1 .... you ever .... India?

2 She .... New York six times.

3 Have you seen my boss? Yes, she .... the bank.

4 Lucky Pia. She's on vacation. She .... Tobago.

5 I .... never .... the Caribbean.

3 Skills work: reading

Put the conversation in the correct order.

.... Well, it was difficult at first but once we got going it
was great, really exciting.

.... Windsurfing, no, but I have been hang gliding.

.... Well, it was hard to land and eventually I hit a tree and
came down with a bump.

.... Oh no, not at all. I'd go again in a second.

.... Let's see ... have you ever done any windsurfing or hang gliding?

.... And you didn't have any problems at all?

.... And that didn't scare you?

.... Sure, go ahead.

...1... I'm doing a survey about dangerous sports. Would you mind if
I asked you a few questions?

.... Really? And how was it?

> **Language note**
> Both *been* and *gone* can be used
> as the past participle of *to be* but
> *been* is more common.
> *Been* means gone and returned:
> He's **been** to Spain twice.
> but *gone* means not yet returned:
> Where's your sister? She's **gone** to
> the movies.
> Remember to use *to* as the
> preposition with the place with
> both *been* and *gone*.

3 Champions' stories

1 Skills work: reading

a Look back at the article in your Student's Book about Michael Schumacher. Underline all the examples of the present perfect and the past simple and think about why they are used in each case.

b The following are the jumbled letters of words from the article. Write the words alongside.

himponca ..champion........

1 g l e r b k o e n (2 words) ....

2 m m c h e o a e (2) ....

3 c h t n c a l e i n w k e d g o l e (2) ....

4 t t n n n c o e o i (1) ....

5 g n l s o i c r a e s (2) ....

c Make sure you know what all these words / phrases mean. Use a dictionary to help.

2 Pronunciation work

Look at these infinitive forms of regular verbs.
Write the past participle (or past simple) form in the correct column, depending on the pronunciation of the final syllable.
Say the verbs to yourself to help you.

> **Language note**
> Remember that the past simple and past participle of regular verbs are the same:
> live   lived   lived
> and that the ending -ed can be pronounced in 3 different ways:
> /d/ /t/ or /id/

| walk   decide   play   camp   climb   study   work   open   close   start   finish |
| free   travel   try   fail   look   visit   listen   want   ask |

/ d /	/ t /	/ id /
played	walked	decided

Can you see any rules which could help you with the pronunciation in the future?

3 Word work: crossword

a Answer the clues and write your answers in the boxes. At the end you should be able to read the key word (one down). All the words are from Unit 10.

						1					
						C	L	I	M	B	E	D

(Crossword grid with numbered cells: 1 (CLIMBED), 2, 3, 4, 5, 6, 7, 8, 9, 10, 11, 12)

Clues

1 Have you ever .... a mountain?

2 A .... is the story of someone's life.

3 I haven't .... to many countries.

4 I've .... in the open several times.

5 He's never .... rugby.

6 She's passed every exam she's taken. She's never .... any.

7 Not married anymore.

8 Sport similar to sailing but for one person. To ....

9 He's started lots of novels but he hasn't .... any of them.

10 How long have you studied .... ?

11 Past participle of *write*.

12 An important moment in your life when things change.

b Now complete these sentences with words from the crossword.

The big .....*turning point*..... in my career was when I got a major part.

1 My marriage didn't work and we got .... in 1998.

2 He was tired after he .... to the seventh story.

3 I've just read this incredible .... of Picasso.

4 I love the sea and I surf a lot, but I don't ....

5 Some historians say that Marco Polo never .... to China.

Unit 11 Ways of life

1 Traditions

Language summary: *make* and *do*				
Use:		**Form:**		
• Use *make* for products, constructions, results: *We **made** a table. They **made** a cake.*		I He	made	a cake for her birthday. a model airplane.

• Use *do* for actions, activities, processes:
  *He **did** his homework. She **did** a good job.*
  But note: *He **made** a phone call.*
		We
		They
			did	our exercises.
				their duty.

1 Language work

Put the correct form of *do* or *make* in the blanks in this text.

I really hate ...*doing*...... the housework. Every day I have to (1) .... breakfast

and then (2) .... the dishes. After that I usually (3) .... the beds. Some days

I also (4) .... the laundry and hang it up to dry.

One thing I can't stand is (5) .... the ironing. My husband always (6) .... that. I like (7) ....

the shopping, though, as it gets me out of the house and I often run into people I know.

When I get back from shopping, I sometimes (8) .... a few phone calls, then I usually (9) ....

dinner and, if I have time, put my feet up before going to pick the children up from school.

2 Skills work: writing

Write a paragraph about what you do every day.
Try to include as many examples of *make* and *do* as you can.

....

....

....

....

....

....

....

3 Skills work: reading

a Read this letter about a trip to New Orleans and then answer the questions.

Dear Nina,

We're having a wonderful time in New Orleans. It's so great to be here during Carnival time or Mardi Gras, as it's called here. There is so much happening in the streets – all sorts of parades and street parties and people wearing fantastic costumes. New Orleans is always lively but at the moment it's even livelier and every night there is so much to choose from – and nearly all of it is free.

Last night we went out for a delicious Cajun (that's a special kind of cooking typical of this region – very hot and spicy!) dinner – shrimp gumbo and blackened chicken! No, really, it was much better than it sounds. After that we went to a great jazz club on the famous Bourbon Street and drank – guess what? – bourbon on the rocks. Tomorrow we're going on a boat trip on the Mississippi – hope I don't fall into a swamp! Then, sadly, it's just one more night and then we have to get on our plane. Anyway that's about it for now. I hope all is well with you and you had a good time in Jamaica. Looking forward to seeing you soon. I'll give you a call when we get back and we can swap vacation pictures!

Lots of love from us both

Carol and Mike

1 What is the relationship between Nina and Carol?

....

2 What is special about Carol's vacation?

....

b Are these statements true or false? Write T for true and F for false.

Carnival in New Orleans is also known as Semana Santa.   ....F....

1 Carol is alone in New Orleans.   ....

2 The streets are lively in New Orleans during Mardi Gras.   ....

3 Cajun food is spicy.   ....

4 Bourbon Street is a well-known street in New Orleans.   ....

5 Carol has one more week in New Orleans.   ....

c Read the letter again and underline all the positive adjectives and the nouns that go with them, e.g. *a wonderful time*. Notice how they are used and think about other nouns you could use with these adjectives.

d Underline words in the letter you are unsure about. Try to guess their meanings. Use a dictionary to check your guesses.

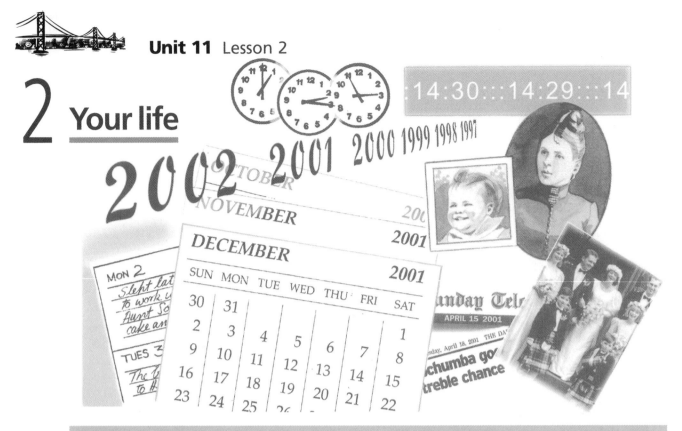

2 Your life

Language summary: talking about actions or states which began in the past and continue now

Use:

Use the present perfect + *for* or *since* to talk about something which began in the past and is still true now. Remember to use *for* with a period of time, *since* with a point in time and *how long* in the question.

How long have you lived here?

We've lived here for two years / since 1999.

Form:

How long	have	you they	lived here?
	has	he she	worked there?
I We They	have	lived here worked there studied English	for a long time. since 1999.
She He	has		

1 Language work

a Put these words / phrases in the correct column, depending on whether they go with *for* or *since*.

| 6 months | 10 years | last week | April | 12 o'clock | a long time | September | 3 weeks |
| Spring | January, 2000 | 1997 | years | 10:30 | this morning | ages | last summer |

For	Since
6 months	last week

66

b **Correct the mistakes.**

How long are you here?

How long have you been here?

1 Oh, since about six months.

....

2 She have live here for one years.

....

3 I study English nine months.

....

4 How long they work there? They work there for 1998.

....

5 We has been in this line 20 minutes.

....

c **Choose the correct one.**

We've been here (since 2 o'clock) / for 2 o'clock.

1 They *have* / *has* lived in Paris for four years.

2 She's *studied* / *studying* English since October.

3 I've been here *since* / *for* three days.

4 He *have* / *has* worked at the college since 1998.

5 We've been in New York *since* / *for* a long time.

6 I've worked here *since* / *for 1981*.

2 Skills work: writing

a **Write five pairs of sentences about yourself, using the present simple and then the present perfect.**

I go to Detroit University. I've studied at the university for 18 months. ....

....

....

....

....

b **Now think of someone you know – a relative or friend – and write five similar pairs of sentences about them.**

....

....

....

....

....

Unit 11 Lesson 3

3 Working together

1 Word work: school regimes

Don't look at your Student's Book. Put these words / phrases in the appropriate column.

| discipline   rank   first names   formality   orders   democratic management   hierarchical structure |
| informal dress   uniforms   creative thinking   raise your hand   open discussion |

Traditional institutions		Modern institutions	
discipline		first names	

Now read the text on Institutional cultures in your Student's Book again to check your answers.

Language summary: reporting orders and requests

Use:				Form:				
• When you want to report orders and requests use *ask want* and *tell*. He **told** me *to clean my boots.* They **asked** him *to leave.*				I She	asked told	him her	to	hurry up. shut the door. do the cleaning.
						them	not to	make a noise. shout.
• Use an object pronoun without *to* after the verb. He **asked her.** I **told him** *to wash the car.* • Remember you can use *not to* after *tell* and *ask* but not usually after *want.* She **told me** / **asked me** *not to hurry.* I **didn't** want *him to leave.*				We	didn't want	him you	to	say anything. watch TV.

2 Language work

a Write these sentences in the correct order.

Make beds he to us our told. <u>He told us to make our beds.</u> ....E..

1 Homework me my to she told do. ....

2 Us they up to stand asked. ....

3 Asked raise hand her her to she. ....

4 Told to us quickly march more he. ....

5 Not boots the leave our told to he us bed under. ....

b Now decide whether the sentences are about school or the army.
Mark each sentence either A (for army) or S (for school) or E (for either).

3 Skills work: reading

a Read this article about a school in Switzerland.

SPRINGFIELD

ONE OF THE MOST PROGRESSIVE SCHOOLS in the world is Springfield. Set in the Swiss countryside in extensive and beautiful grounds, Springfield is a very special school indeed. It is a private boarding school and parents pay high fees to send their children there. At Springfield, students are on a first-name basis with their teachers and they study subjects which are different from those at other schools such as jewelry making and unusual languages. But by far the most exceptional thing about Springfield is that the staff does not tell the students what to do – they do not even tell them to attend classes. This is a matter of choice. Many people have criticized Springfield for having no discipline and for failing to give children a proper start in life. But there is a very important principle behind letting them choose whether to attend classes or not. The belief is that this, in fact, gives them a much greater sense of responsibility, and a healthier and more positive attitude towards their education. In this way, according to staff at Springfield, children are much better prepared for real life than they would be at a more orthodox school.

b Write complete sentences and use your own words as much as possible.

1 What is special about Springfield?

....

....

2 Why do people criticize Springfield?

....

....

3 What is the philosophy behind the way Springfield is organized?

....

....

c Find words / phrases in the article which mean the same as the following:

modern	residential school ....
address by their first name	very unusual ....
teachers	optional ....
appropriate	belief ....
feeling of being in control	traditional ....

Now use a dictionary to check your answers.

Unit 12 What's next?

1 Reviewing the situation

ə ʌ θ æ ŋ ʃ

1 Pronunciation work

a Look at these words from this and earlier units. Underline the stressed syllable.

<u>da</u>ting   <u>dic</u>tionary   <u>se</u>rious   <u>ear</u>ly   fif<u>teen</u>
questionn<u>aire</u>   information   windsurfing   engaged
television   kitchen   prisoner   thirty   later   waiter
rarely   neighbor   graduation   commercial   fairly
displays   celebrations   parades   picnics   painting
cafeteria   parents   purses   ambition   history   witness
difficulty   favorite   tuition   freedom   teenagers
wavy   appearance   e-mail   museum   admission

day	sit
dating	dictionary

be	girl	share	ear		
fifteen	early	questionnaire	serious		

b Now put the words in the correct column depending on the sound of the stressed syllable. Check that you know what all the words mean.

Language summary: past simple vs. present perfect				
Use:	**Form:**			
• Remember to use the past simple + *ago* to talk about something which happened at a specific time in the past. *I **started** college four years **ago**.*	I She	came here	six years ago.	
• Use the present perfect + *for* or *since* to talk about something which started in the past and continues in the present. *He's **lived** in this apartment **for** six months / **since** January.*	He They	's 've	worked there	since last fall. for ten months.

2 Language work

Rewrite these sentences using the present perfect + *for*.

I moved to this house five weeks ago.

 I've lived in this house for five weeks. ....

1 She emigrated to Texas a year ago.

....

2 She started her job two years ago.

....

3 They left for their vacation ten days ago.

....

4 My brother started studying English six months ago.

....

5 I came here a week ago.

....

3 Skills work: reading and writing

a **Read the questionnaire in your Student's Book again, and the text about Helen and Peter.**

b **Write a paragraph about yourself and the things which have or have not changed for you. Use the prompts to help you.**

Ten years ago ....

and / but ....

Five years ago ....

and / but ....

A year ago ....

and / but ....

2 Immediate plans

Language summary: talking about future plans			
Use:	**Form:**		
• Use *going to* + the infinitive without *to* for a definite plan or intention. *I'm **going to learn** Italian.*	I'm We're	going to	learn Chinese.
• Use the present continuous for an arrangement (usually involving someone else). *I'm **meeting** my sister for lunch.*	He's She's	leaving	tomorrow. tonight.
• Use *might* + the infinitive without *to* for a possible future plan, something which is not definite. *We **might visit** the islands. It depends on the weather.*	I They	might	visit the islands.

1 Language work

a **Correct the mistakes.**

I'm going cycle to school. *I'm going to cycle to school.* ....

1 She going to watch TV this evening. ....

2 I might to go to a movie. ....

3 They go for a drink tomorrow night. ....

4 We going learn German. ....

5 He might leaving college. ....

b **Look at these two pages of Becky's diary. Write 8 sentences about Becky's plans for the next two weeks. Use *going to* for a plan / intention and the present continuous for an arrangement with someone else. Where the day is blank, use *might* and invent some ideas of your own. The first three have been done for you.**

1 MONDAY	MONDAY 8
dentist	back to work!
2 TUESDAY	TUESDAY 9
Emily / lunch	dinner with Mom
3 WEDNESDAY	WEDNESDAY 10
4 THURSDAY	THURSDAY 11
drink STEVE	eye doctor 5.30 p.m.
5 FRIDAY	FRIDAY 12
Sarah's party	movies Sarah
6 SATURDAY	SATURDAY 13
shopping – new dress	take it easy!
7 SUNDAY	SUNDAY 14
start jogging!	

She's going to the dentist on Monday.
On Tuesday she's meeting Emily for lunch.
On Wednesday she might go out or she might stay home.

1 ....
2 ....
3 ....
4 ....
5 ....
6 ....
7 ....
8 ....

2 Skills work: writing

a Rearrange these words / phrases to make questions.

might take / after this one / do you think / you / another English course / ?
 Do you think you might take another English course after this one?

1 tonight / to do / going / what are you / ?

....

2 on vacation / you going / soon / are / ?

....

3 your family / in the next month / is / planning to celebrate / anything special / ?

....

4 next weekend / are you / what / doing / ?

....

5 at the end / do you think / of this English course / what / you will do / ?

....

b Write a paragraph about your plans for the near future – next month, your next vacation,
next weekend, etc. Try to use a mixture of *going to*, the present progressive and *might*.

....
....
....
....
....
....

3 Twenty-five years from now

1 Word work 1: life in the future

a Look at these words / phrases about the future. Put them in the correct column.

| VCRs   slums   cable TV   overpopulation   literacy rates   the Internet   medical care |
| nuclear power   life expectancy   e-mail   immigration   fiber optics   global warming |

Social / environmental issues		Technological advances	
slums		VCRs	

b Use a dictionary to check you know what all these words / phrases mean.

Language summary: making predictions about the future

Use:	Form:			
Use *will* or *won't* (*will not*) + the infinitive without *to* for making predictions about the future.	It	will	get	hotter.
				wetter.
There **will be** more people living in cities.	It	won't		cooler.
Conditions in cities **won't** improve.	Oil			cheaper.

2 Skills work: writing

a Look at these sentences. Put a check (✓) in the circle you think most appropriate.

	Definitely	Maybe	Definitely not
The population will increase in cities and decrease in the country.	✓	○	○
1 The earth will continue to get warmer and weather conditions will change.	○	○	○
2 Public transportation won't improve.	○	○	○
3 People will live in complexes which include stores, offices, etc.	○	○	○
4 Most shopping will be done on the Internet.	○	○	○
5 Most people won't go to work, but will work from home.	○	○	○
6 People won't work so much and will have more leisure time.	○	○	○

b Now use your answers to write a paragraph about how you see the future.
Use *will* and *won't* and add some ideas of your own.

....

....

....

....

3 Word work 2: general review

Make your own mini-glossary.
Try to write ten words / phrases under each heading. Do this as fast as you can. Try to do it from memory,
but if it's too difficult, look at the Student's Book to help you.

housing	transportation	vacation / travel	education	relationships

crime	culture / festivals	health / fitness	work	entertainment / sports

A Learner training

1 Recording and remembering vocabulary

It is a good idea to buy a separate notebook to write vocabulary in. The vocabulary in this Workbook and the Student's Book are recorded in different ways to help you remember new words. Experiment by using these different methods in your notebook.

1 Words in columns:

Country	Nationality	Language
Mexico	Mexican	Spanish
Canada	Canadian	English/French
Austria	Austrian	German

2 Words in lists, for example using opposites or synonyms:

Word	Opposite
hot	cold
clean	dirty
big	small

3 Spidergrams

4 Drawing the objects.

Task 1

What do you think is the best way to record these groups of words? Write columns, list or spidergram next to each one.

1 Rooms in a house, types of furniture, types of house – spidergram
2 Verb + noun pairs: *eat + fish, study + Spanish*
3 School subjects, people who study / specialize in that subject
4 Adjectives + comparative forms
5 Jobs, places of work, things in an office

2 More ways of recording and remembering vocabulary

When you want to record a new word or phrase, either from the book or from somewhere else, it is a good idea to include a definition or a sentence to help you remember what it means and / or a translation.

table   mesa
filing cabinet A piece of furniture, often found in an office, for storing files
stressful   My job is very stressful at the moment – I have so much work these days!

It is also a good idea to include the part of speech and the stress. Write down difficult pronunciation too.

table (n) <u>ta</u>ble

Task 2

Record these words using as many of the ideas above as you can.

1 factory
2 twice
3 handsome
4 attend
5 occasionally

3 Reviewing and recycling new words and phrases

Once you have recorded your new words and phrases, it is a good idea to keep reviewing and recycling them so that you really remember them. For example, you can:

- learn 10 new words / phrases a week.
- test yourself by covering up the definition / picture.
- write a sentence including each new word.
- write a paragraph or story including a number of new words / phrases.

Suggested answers

Task 2	Task 1
1 factory (n) A place where things are made / manufactured. fabrica	1 spidergram
2 twice (adv) Two times / dos veces	2 list
3 handsome (adj) Good looking (usually for a man).	3 columns
4 attend (vb) I attend college every day	4 list
5 occasionally (adv) The opposite of "often" – We occasionally go to the movies.	5 spidergram

B Spelling rules

Rule 1 Contractions

In English, it is common to use contractions, especially with verb forms. An apostrophe is used to show where letters are missing in the contracted forms. Contractions are used mainly in speech but you will also see them in written English, particularly when the style is informal.

he is	he's
we are	we're
I am	I'm
she has been	she's been
they have been	they've been

we also contract *not* to -*n't*

she is not	she isn't
they do not	they don't
you cannot	you can't
I have not been	I haven't been

Task 1

Write the contracted forms.

1 you are ....

2 we do not ....

3 she must not ....

4 it is ....

5 he does not ....

Rule 2 Apostrophes to indicate possession

We use an apostrophe with a name to indicate possession:
John's book.
Be careful not to confuse '*s* to indicate possession with the contraction of the verb *to be*.
Pedro's bicycle = the bicycle that **belongs** to Pedro.
Pedro's a doctor = Pedro **is** a doctor.

Task 2

Put the following in the correct column.

is	belongs to

1 Jack's a computer programmer.

2 Susana's sister lives in Montreal.

3 Celia's house is in the city center.

4 Gianni's tall and slim.

5 Christine's a teacher.

Rule 3 Plurals

- To form the plural of nouns, we normally add "-s":
  a table – two tables, a girl – girls
- If the noun ends in "-y" after a consonant, change the "-y" to "-ie" and add "-s":
  a city – a number of cities, a country – two countries
- Some plurals are irregular:
  woman – women, man – men, child – children

Rule 4 Verbs: present simple

- For most forms of the present simple, use the infinitive form:
  I go, we see, they learn
- For the third person singular, add "-s":
  she thinks, he lives
- For verbs ending in "-y" after a consonant, change the "-y" to "-ie" and add "-s":
  he studies, she tries
- For verbs ending in "-sh" or "-ch", add "-es":
  she teaches, he washes

Language note
Note the following irregular verbs.
she goes, he does, she has

Language note
Uncountable nouns do not take a plural form.
Cheese is nice ✔
Cheeses are nices ✘

Language note
Adjectives do not take a plural form.
a *nice* boy ✔
two *nice* boys ✔
two *nices* boys ✘

Task 3

Write the third person singular (with *he* or *she*) of these verbs:

1 work
2 watch
3 cry
4 finish
5 leave

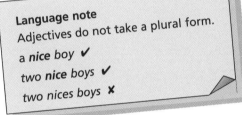

Answers

works, watches, cries, finishes, leaves

Task 3

belongs to: 2, 3

is: 1, 4, 5

Task 2

you're, we don't, she mustn't, it's, he doesn't

Task 1

Macmillan Publishers
Between Towns Road, Oxford OX4 3PP
A division of Macmillan Publishers Limited
Companies and representatives throughout the world

ISBN-13 : 987 0 333 92675 8
Text © Macmillan Publishers Limited 2001

Design and illustration © Macmillan Publishers Limited 2001

First published 2001

Designed by Oliver Hickey

Illustrated by Martin Aston, Andy Warrington, Geoff Waterhouse and
Maureen Gray.

Cover photograph by Stone

The authors and publishers would like to thank the following for
permission to reproduce their material:
Maya Jaggi "Life at a Glance" from The Guardian 30.9.00 © The
Guardian 2000, reprinted by permission of Guardian Newspapers Ltd

The authors and publishers would like to thank the following for permission
to reproduce their photographs:
Corbis pp15 (Nik Wheeler), 28 (Pawel Libera), 47 (Owen Franken), 58
(Rune Hellestad); Image Bank p12; Stone pp6, 9, 10, 22, 42, 49, 53, 65, 69

Printed in Thailand

2011 2010 2009 2008 2007
16 15 14 13 12 11 10